EVERYDAY
STEM

LIGHT

Patricia Hutchison and John Willis

AV2

www.av2books.com

Step 1
Go to **www.av2books.com**

Step 2
Enter this unique code

Step 3
Explore your interactive eBook!

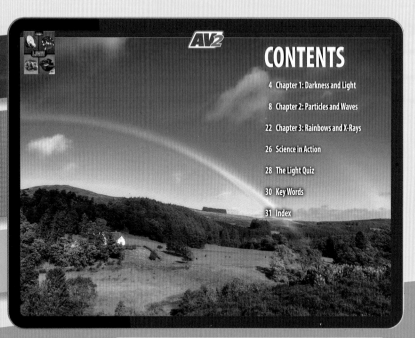

CONTENTS

AV2 is optimized for use on any device

Your interactive eBook comes with...

Contents
Browse a live contents page to easily navigate through resources

Audio
Listen to sections of the book read aloud

Videos
Watch informative video clips

Weblinks
Gain additional information for research

Try This!
Complete activities and hands-on experiments

Key Words
Study vocabulary, and complete a matching word activity

Quizzes
Test your knowledge

Slideshows
View images and captions

... and much, much more!

Everything looks black. The electricity is off. After a few minutes, the lamp flickers back on. The objects in the room are now visible. Everything is colorful again.

Light is the opposite of darkness. Light is what makes colors possible. Without light, our eyes would not work. That is why the room looked black when the lamp went out.

Reading in dim light can make your eyes tire quickly.

Everyday STEM

Particles and Waves

All objects give off and take in **electromagnetic waves**. There are many types of these waves. Humans cannot see most of them. These types of waves include X-rays, radio waves, and many others.

Holiday lights give off colors with different wavelengths.

The waves humans can see are known as the visible **spectrum**. These waves also have a simpler name. They are called light.

Each color in the visible spectrum has a different **wavelength**. A wavelength is the length of one complete cycle of a wave. The colors in the visible spectrum have very short wavelengths. The wavelengths are so small they are **microscopic**.

Other wavelengths can be much longer. For example, radio wavelengths can be hundreds of feet long.

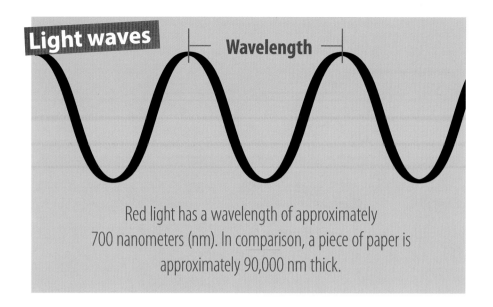

Light waves

Wavelength

Red light has a wavelength of approximately 700 nanometers (nm). In comparison, a piece of paper is approximately 90,000 nm thick.

Electromagnetic waves carry energy. The waves are sometimes called rays or beams. They are made up of tiny particles called **photons**.

All colors travel at approximately the same speed in air. They travel slower in water or glass. Red light has the longest wavelength of the colors in the rainbow. Violet light has the shortest wavelength. Red light moves more quickly through water than violet light does.

THE ELECTROMAGNETIC SPECTRUM

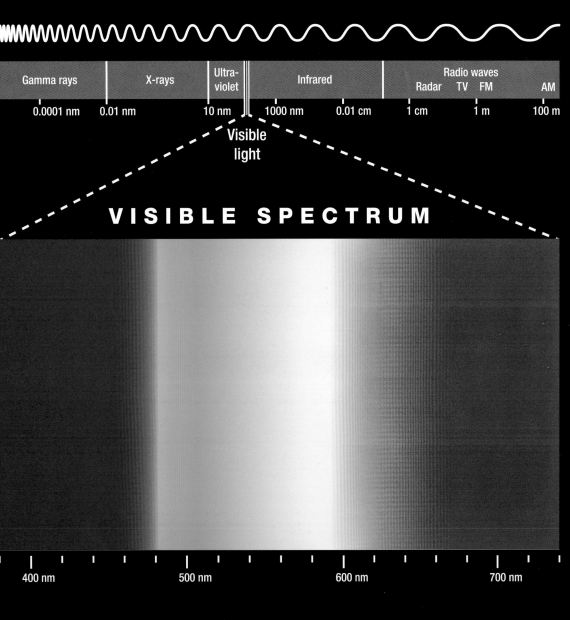

Gamma rays		X-rays		Ultra-violet		Infrared			Radio waves			
								Radar	TV	FM		AM
0.0001 nm	0.01 nm			10 nm		1000 nm	0.01 cm	1 cm		1 m		100 m

Visible
light

VISIBLE SPECTRUM

400 nm   500 nm   600 nm   700 nm

Pumpkins absorb most light but reflect orange light.

Light rays usually move in a straight line. These rays hit objects in their path. An object usually absorbs some of the light that hits it. The rest of the light may **reflect** off the object.

Every object reflects light differently. That is why different objects are different colors. For example, a pumpkin reflects more orange light. A banana reflects more yellow light.

A black object absorbs most of the light that hits it. A white object does the opposite. It reflects most of the light that hits it.

A shiny surface also reflects most light. A mirror is one example. A mirror appears different from a white object, however. That is because a mirror's surface is very smooth.

Many objects do not allow light to pass through them. That is why they cast shadows.

A mirror reflects most of the light that hits its surface.

A heated horseshoe gives off light.

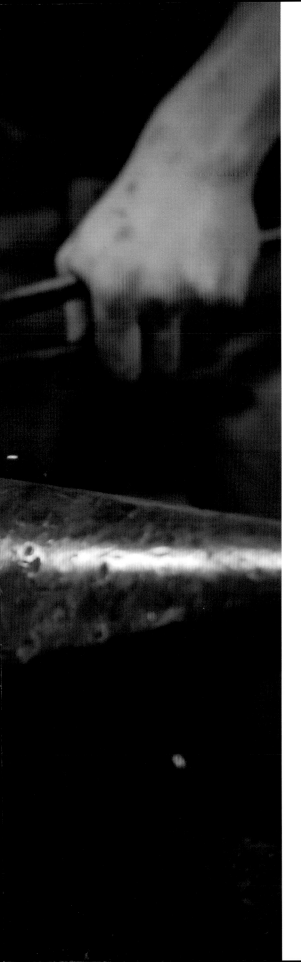

Light can pass through some objects. For example, light can pass through a thin sheet of paper. Light can also pass through glass and some types of plastic.

Objects may give off light when they are very hot. The Sun is one example. It is a star. It gives off light and other electromagnetic waves. These waves have energy. The energy makes life on Earth possible.

Light rays can also bend, or **refract**. This happens when light moves through one transparent substance to another. For example, air and water are two substances we can see through.

Suppose light rays move from the air into water. The light rays will slow down and change direction. That is why a straw looks broken when it is in a glass of water.

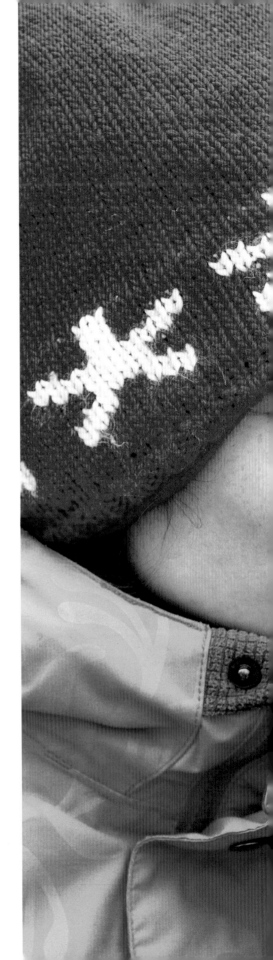

Straws appear to bend in water because light rays are being refracted.

Rainbows and X-Rays

A rainbow shows the colors of the visible spectrum. The light from the Sun moves through the air. Then, it moves through millions of raindrops. The light is refracted. It is separated into seven colors. They are red, orange, yellow, green, blue, indigo, and violet. When your back is to the Sun, your eyes see the colorful rainbow across the sky.

RIGHT

Doctors have been using
X-rays for more than a century.

X-rays are part of the electromagnetic spectrum humans cannot see. Doctors find X-rays useful. They use a machine to pass an X-ray beam through the body. The rays travel easily through skin and muscle. Bones absorb the rays. The bones cast a white shadow on the film used to capture the rays. Doctors can see a picture of the bone to tell if it is broken.

Making a Color Wheel

What would you see if you mixed the colors of the rainbow together? Do this experiment to find out. Be sure to get help from an adult.

STEP 1 Draw a circle on a piece of poster board. Carefully cut out the circle.

STEP 2 Use a pencil to lightly divide the circle into six equal parts, similar to a pie.

STEP 3 Color each space in this order: yellow, orange, red, purple, blue, and green.

STEP 4 Push a thumbtack through the center of your color wheel. Pin the wheel to the top of a pencil's eraser.

STEP 5 Put the pencil between your palms. Slide your palms back and forth. Spin the pencil as fast as you can. Watch what happens to the color wheel. What color did you see? Is this the color you thought you would see? How can you explain what happened? What do you think would happen if you put the colors in a different order on your color wheel?

THE LIGHT QUIZ

- 1 -
What is the opposite of darkness?

A. Light

- 2 -
What is another name for the light we can see?

A. Visible spectrum

- 3 -
What color of light does a pumpkin mainly reflect?

A. Orange

- 4 -
What tiny particles make up electromagnetic waves?

A. Photons

- 5 -
Which color has the shortest wavelength?

A. Violet

- 6 -
Why does a mirror reflect most light?

A. Its surface is very smooth

- 7 -
Do black or white objects absorb more light?

A. Black

- 8 -
What are the seven colors of the rainbow?

A. Red, orange, yellow, green, blue, indigo, violet

- 9 -
Can light pass through glass?

A. Yes

- 10 -
How do light waves change when they refract?

A. They bend

Key Words

electromagnetic waves: waves that have both electric and magnetic properties

microscopic: too small to see without a microscope

photons: particles that make up light rays

reflect: to bounce off something

refract: to change the direction of a wave when it passes from one material into another

spectrum: a range that changes gradually from one end to the other

wavelength: the length of one cycle, or one complete repetition, of a wave

Index

Get the best of both worlds.

AV2 bridges the gap between print and digital.

The expandable resources toolbar enables quick access to content including **videos**, **audio**, **activities**, **weblinks**, **slideshows**, **quizzes**, and **key words**.

Animated videos make static images come alive.

Resource icons on each page help readers to further **explore key concepts**.

Published by AV2
14 Penn Plaza, 9th Floor New York, NY 10122
Website: www.av2books.com

Library of Congress Control Number: 2020936967

ISBN 978-1-7911-2380-2 (hardcover)
ISBN 978-1-7911-2381-9 (softcover)
ISBN 978-1-7911-2382-6 (multi-user eBook)
ISBN 978-1-7911-2383-3 (single-user eBook)

Printed in Guangzhou, China
1 2 3 4 5 6 7 8 9 0   24 23 22 21 20

052020
101319

Designer: Terry Paulhus Project Coordinator: Priyanka Das

Every reasonable effort has been made to trace ownership and to obtain permission to reprint copyright material. The publisher would be pleased to have any errors or omissions brought to its attention so that they may be corrected in subsequent printings.

The publisher acknowledges Getty Images, iStock, and Shutterstock as its primary image suppliers for this title.

First published by Focus Readers in 2018.